D0371462

Everyday Prayers
for
Everyday Cares

f o r   M o t h e r s

Honor Books
Tulsa, Oklahoma

Everyday Prayers for Everyday Cares for Mothers
ISBN 1-56292-539-3
Copyright © 2002 by Honor Books
P.O. Box 55388
Tulsa, Oklahoma 74155

Manuscript written by Vicki Kuyper, Colorado Springs, Colorado.

Introduction

Women lead busy lives and fill many roles. But regardless of whether they spend their days in the garden or the nursery or the boardroom, one thing is certain: their days are often filled with cares, frustrations, and responsibilities.

Everyday Prayers for Everyday Cares for Mothers is designed to remind you that God is able—able to handle every problem, no matter how great, no matter how seemingly insignificant. The simple prayers and selected scriptures are meant to encourage and uplift you as they urge you to invite God into your day. And the prayers have been placed in categories so that you can find exactly what you need when you need it.

May God richly bless you as you apply these simple prayers to the cares you face each day.

Many women do noble things, but you surpass them all.

PROVERBS 31:29

Contents

When

I FEEL AFRAID . . .

Hide me under the shadow of Your wings.

PSALM 17:8 NKJV

FATHER,

Your presence provides a haven of comfort.

There are times when I want to hide from the world. Everything seems too big, too hard, too much. But, You are like a mother bird tending her young. I have found a safe place beneath Your wings. What a beautiful picture of Your gentle care! Thank You for not making me feel ashamed of being afraid but instead offering me a place of peace. Hold me close. Show me how much bigger You are than what I'm afraid of.

Amen.

God is the strength of my heart.

FATHER,

You calm my heart.

It isn't only children who are afraid of monsters. Fear grows inside me over the smallest things. Help me see what I'm afraid of through Your eyes, instead of with my own fearful heart. Give me the confidence to move forward in Your strength, not my own. Bring to mind the fears You've helped me face in the past; then help me face this with my head held high—not because I'm brave, but because of Your power in my life.

Amen.

Let the beloved of the LORD rest secure in him.

DEUTERONOMY 33:12

FATHER,

You offer me rest in the safety of Your love.

Nothing can happen to me or my children that will separate us from Your love. Why should I be afraid? You know the past and the future. Your hand is on the present. Just knowing that there is nothing in this life that I will face alone takes away so many fears I have as a parent. Thank You for turning my fears into yet another reason to praise You. You truly are a Worker of miracles.

Amen.

I can do everything through him who gives me strength.

PHILIPPIANS 4:13

FATHER,

You give me courage.

Sometimes being a mom is downright scary. I'm overwhelmed by my responsibilities and my own limitations. You know what lies ahead of me, and only You know how afraid I really am. Help me do what I have to do. I want to be strong, but I don't want to rely solely on myself. Thank You for showing me how weak I am without You and how strong I am with You by my side.

Amen.

• • •

When

I FEEL ALONE . . .

Do not be far from me, for trouble is near and there is no one to help.

PSALM 22:11

FATHER,

You are always by my side.

Right now I feel as though You are so far away, but I know that's only my lonely heart speaking. Please drown out its voice with Your love. Draw me close to Your side. Give me a sense of Your presence. Keep reminding me that even when I feel lonely, I am never alone because You are always with me. You are right here in this room, whispering words of love and encouragement. Help quiet my heart so that I am able to hear them.

Amen.

*How precious it is, Lord, to realize that you
are thinking about me constantly!*

FATHER,

You have me on Your mind.

Even when I feel forgotten by the world, You call me by name. You care about every detail of my day. All of my friends seem so preoccupied with their own lives. I understand, but it leaves me feeling so lonely. Thank You for never forgetting me or deserting me, for never having so many things on Your To Do list that I drop to the bottom. Thanks for thinking about me today and every day. It makes me feel so loved!

Amen.

Do all that is in your heart, for God is with you.

1 CHRONICLES 17:2 NKJV

FATHER,

You don't let me give up.

In every aspect of parenting—every decision I make, every lesson I try to teach, every time I have to discipline my kids—You're beside me. You never let me fight a battle or celebrate a victory alone. You're there cheering me on, giving me wisdom, and showering our family with Your never-ending love. That's what gives me the strength to keep going. Thank You for putting a song in my heart, even when parenting is tough.

Amen.

You are the helper of the fatherless.

PSALM 10:14

FATHER,

You come alongside me as I parent.

Thank You for being there for my children. I know that no matter how good of a mother I am, I'll never be able to meet every one of my children's needs. But with You by my side, I know I can be the mother You designed me to be. And that is enough. That's all You ask. Even when I feel like I'm facing this job of parenting all alone, You are faithful to provide the help I need physically, emotionally, and spiritually.

Amen.

•   •   •

When

I FEEL ANGRY . . .

Be careful that when you get on each other's nerves you don't snap at each other.

1 THESSALONIANS 5:15 THE MESSAGE

FATHER,

You help me hold my tongue.

You know exactly what's going on in my mind. You know that even though I love my kids, the words that spring to my lips when I get angry with them are far from loving. Please help me stop and think before I speak. Reveal to me what's behind my anger, whether I'm feeling inconvenienced, taken for granted, embarrassed, or just plain grouchy. Don't let me react to their anger with anger of my own. Teach me to love, no matter what the circumstance.

Amen.

Do not let the sun go down while you are still angry.

EPHESIANS 4:26

FATHER,

You help me let go of my bitterness.

The events of the day keep running through my head. I can't seem to let go of the anger, but I know You want me to. Help me place my hurt, my disappointment, and even my rage into Your mighty hands. Fill my mind with good things and reasons for praise, instead of my list of how I've been wronged. Then give me the courage to make things right with my kids, even if I'm not the one who is in the wrong.

Amen.

A tenderhearted person lives a blessed life.

PROVERBS 28:14 THE MESSAGE

FATHER,

You make my angry heart tender again.

You know just how to transform an angry heart—and home. Bless me with more than just self-control. Change me from the inside out. Help me pull out the roots of my anger and deal with them. Please replace them with a spirit of gentleness, peace, forgiveness, and reconciliation. Make my heart and home a place where You would be happy to live. Forgive me for where my anger has led me. Lead me back to You and Your loving arms.

Amen.

Do not let any unwholesome talk come out of your mouths, but only what is helpful for building others up.

FATHER,

You give me words that heal instead of hurt.

You are the Creator of speech and the ultimate Master over it. You know where I am weak and need Your wisdom, especially when I'm angry. I know You will continue to purify my heart and my words as I grow closer to You. May every word I give to my children be a gift. Keep me from letting things slip from my mouth that would wound them, discourage them, or make them feel like less than the beloved miracles they truly are.

Amen.

•   •   •

When

I FEEL ANXIOUS . . .

---

*The LORD is faithful to all his promises and
loving toward all he has made.*

PSALM 145:13

FATHER,

You remain faithful.

There is nothing in this life that You and I can't handle.
When my heart fails, bring to my mind the power of that
truth. Unlike me, You always keep Your promises. You've
promised to love my kids and me no matter what. Help
my heart rest in that love. Stop my anxious thoughts.
Take me in Your arms, just as I do my own kids, and let
me know that everything will be ok.

Amen.

Think about things that are pure and lovely,
and dwell on the fine, good things in others.

PHILIPPIANS 4:8 TLB

FATHER,

You help me dwell on good things.

Sometimes my thoughts run away with me. The struggles with my kids seem to overshadow the blessings of parenting. My weaknesses loom larger than the victories You've brought into my life. Help me turn my thoughts around. Take my eyes off of the obstacles and focus them toward a clearer picture of You and Your love. Let me see my children the way You do. Encourage me with the promise of what lies ahead. Remind me of just how good You are.

Amen.

I the LORD do not change.

FATHER,

You are my Rock.

There's nothing I can depend on in life besides You. My kids, my spouse, and my friends will all let me down. And I'll do the same thing to them. When I trust something or someone to remain as steadfast as You, I'll always be disappointed. It will always make me feel anxious. The only One I can count on to remain true, immovable, and faithful is You. Your love remains the same, no matter what the circumstances.

Amen.

May God bless you richly and grant you increasing freedom from all anxiety and fear.

1 PETER 1:2 TLB

FATHER,

You set me free.

My anxious thoughts feel like heavy chains weighing me down. Everything seems harder than it has to be. And, somehow, I seem smaller than ever. During times like this, help me see how big You really are. My God and my King, all of my fears and worries pale when I place them in Your mighty hands. I want to do that right now. I give them all to You. Help me live in the freedom You've promised me.

Amen.

• • •

When
I FEEL BLESSED . . .

I'm singing at the top of my lungs, I'm so full of answered prayers.

PSALM 13:6 THE MESSAGE

FATHER,

You are the Reason I feel blessed.

It isn't luck, hard work, or fate. It's You, Father, and Your love for me that has filled my heart with such joy. I know You hear every prayer, but seeing how You've chosen to answer this one makes me smile. Your timing is always perfect. Thanks for listening, caring, and providing in ways I never even would have thought of. You truly are a creative God! Don't let me forget what You've done for our family today.

Amen.

Every good and perfect gift is from above, coming down from the Father of the heavenly lights.

FATHER,

You are the Source of every gift.

"Thank You" seems so small in light of what You've done. Open my eyes to the little things I overlook, to the blessings I take for granted each and every day. Teach me how to model a gratitude attitude for my children. Fill this home with thankful hearts that reflect Your generosity to each of us. You know just what we need. And You always know the perfect way to fill those needs. Thank You! Thank You! Thank You!

Amen.

This is the day the LORD has made; let us rejoice and be glad in it.

PSALM 118:24

FATHER,

You planned it all.

You knew today was coming, and You knew just how it would delight my heart. Thank You for all You've done to make today worth celebrating. Let my joy overflow into the lives of those around me. Let my thanks to You come in shouts, instead of whispers. When the hard days come, remind me of today. Remind me that Your love is as strong for me in that moment as it is right now.

Amen.

A longing fulfilled is sweet to the soul.

PROVERBS 13:19

FATHER,

You are worthy of praise.

Your abundance makes every day feel a bit like Thanksgiving. You know what my heart longs for and exactly what to do to fill those longings. Your answers to prayer don't always look like what I have in mind, but I trust Your plan and Your love for me. You desire for me to be whole, to be changed. Thank You for all of the blessings You bestow along the way, just because You love me.

Amen.

•   •   •

When

I NEED COMFORT . . .

You keep track of all my sorrows. You have collected all my tears in your bottle. You have recorded each one in your book.

PSALM 56:8 NLT

FATHER,

You are only a prayer away.

Today has been one long prayer. What I long to do is curl up under the covers and have a good cry. But You've made me a mom, and I know there are things I have to do. Important things. Help me see how what I do really does matter. But most of all, help me see how much I matter to You. Give me insight into the tears that keep escaping. Thanks for keeping track of each one.

Amen.

"I know the plans I have for you," declares the LORD, *"plans to prosper you and not to harm you, plans to give you hope and a future."*

JEREMIAH 29:11

FATHER,

You have a plan for me.

Nothing happens to me that You don't know about. Right now I don't understand Your plan for me; it hurts too much to even try. But I trust in Your love. I know You're leading me toward a future that You alone have designed to draw me closer to You. You know that's what my heart truly longs for. Help me not to lose hope when life hurts, but instead help me catch sight of Your hand in the midst of all things.

Amen.

You are my God! Hour by hour I place my days in your hand.

PSALM 31:14-15 THE MESSAGE

FATHER,

You are the One I need to turn to.

But You know where I go . . . to the pantry for a snack, to the TV for diversion, to the phone for mindless conversation, to the mall to buy things I don't need. What I really need is You. But You're often the last one I turn to. Forgive me for continuing to run away. Show me the emptiness of the things I reach to for comfort instead of You. Help me hold You as closely as You do me.

Amen.

You will keep in perfect peace him whose mind is steadfast, because he trusts in you.

ISAIAH 26:3

FATHER,

You dry my tears from within.

I feel as though my heart is broken. But You're the Healer of hearts, the Mender of wounds. Be my Refuge right now. Let Your love flow over me, soothing the ache inside that nothing else can touch. Restore to me a sense of peace through the power of Your healing presence. I trust in Your timing. I'll stay in this valley until You lead me out of it. You're my Comfort and my Peace, no matter what the circumstance.

Amen.

•   •   •

When

I AM CONFUSED . . .

Knowledge of the Holy One results in under-standing.

PROVERBS 9:10 NLT

FATHER,

Your truth sets things straight.

There are so many gray areas in parenting. Everyone seems to have advice on how to "do it right," yet even the experts disagree. Lord, You're the only "Expert" I can truly rely on. Only You can teach me how to really love my kids in a way that will help them mature in a Godly manner. The closer I get to You, the wiser I'll be as a parent. Show me how to do both.

Amen.

You are my rock and my fortress; Therefore, for Your name's sake, Lead me and guide me.

PSALM 31:3 NKJV

FATHER,

You help me make wise decisions.

You promise to lead me and guide me. Fulfill that promise now, Lord. I need Your wisdom to know where to turn and what to do. When there isn't a definite right or wrong, sometimes it's hard to commit to a decision. But I need to. Please lead me to Your word in the Bible or people who can give me wise counsel in this area. Then, give my heart the assurance I need to move forward in faith.

Amen.

Show me where to walk, for I have come to you in prayer.

PSALM 143:8 NLT

FATHER,

You show me what my next step should be.

I've come to You in prayer because I don't know where to turn. I'm so overwhelmed I hardly even know where to start. Clear my mind of everything except what I need to deal with right now. Help me put aside the big picture and deal with today, this hour, this moment. Help me prioritize what I need to do in light of Your commands. Then give me the resolve, clarity, and wisdom that I need to take action.

Amen.

May the Lord of peace Himself give you peace always in every way.

2 THESSALONIANS 3:16 NKJV

FATHER,

You quiet my mind with Your truth.

My life feels like it's caught in a whirlwind, but You are the Eye of the storm. Be my Peace. When nothing else seems to make sense, be my Touchstone of truth. Help me to order my thoughts and toss out the ones that do nothing but stir up dissension in my spirit and in my home. Turn every worry and every question into a prayer. Then, help me bring it to Your throne in humility, seeking Your wisdom above the world's.

Amen.

•   •   •

When

I FEEL DEPRESSED . . .

> *Why are you down in the dumps, dear soul?*
> *Why are you crying the blues? Fix my eyes on*
> *God—soon I'll be praising again.*

PSALM 43:5 THE MESSAGE

FATHER,

You give me cause for praise.

Nothing is really wrong, but life just doesn't feel right. Joy seems so far away. I know that my mood not only affects me, but also my kids. Lead me out from under this black cloud into a place of praise. Help me remember the prayers You've answered, the miracles You've worked in the Bible and in my own life. Turn my tears to songs of worship. Only You have the power to lift my heavy heart to Heaven.

Amen.

Enjoy the company of ordinary people.

ROMANS 12:16 NLT

FATHER,

You provide a circle of friends.

Thank You for the friends You've given me. Help me to be honest with them about how I feel. You've designed me for companionship, not only with You, but also with those You've given me to love. When depression takes hold, it's so easy for me to hide within myself. Draw me out. Help me let others love me. Show me how to accept their comfort and prayers without playing the martyr. Use them to draw me closer to You.

Amen.

Give thanks in all circumstances, for this is God's will for you in Christ Jesus.

1 THESSALONIANS 5:18

FATHER,

You help me see the bigger picture.

The more I look at the struggles in my life, the deeper the hole I seem to dig myself into. Gratitude seems like the last thing I could find in my heart right now. But in Your wisdom, You tell me to look deeper. Help me see the blessings You continue to bring to my family, even when I'm downright ungrateful. Show me the good You're bringing about, even when things seem so bad. Create in me a thankful heart.

Amen.

You are my place of refuge. You are all I really want in life.

PSALM 142:5 NLT

FATHER,

You are my Refuge.

You know every dark place in my heart. When I find myself hiding there, You never hesitate to join me in the middle of the pain. Thank You for walking beside me through the valleys of my life. You're my constant, loving Companion. Shine the light of truth onto the lies I cling to. I don't want to dwell there any longer. I want to walk with confidence through every circumstance because You, the God of the universe, cherish me.

Amen.

•   •   •

When

I Feel Discouraged . . .

We fix our eyes not on what is seen, but on what is unseen.

2 Corinthians 4:18

Father,

You help me see with my heart.

I'm so distracted and discouraged by what I see with my eyes, but I know there is more to life than what I see. Help me look beyond the circumstances around me to what You're doing in my children's hearts, as well as in my own. I know that You're conforming us into the image of Your Son. That can't happen overnight or without a fight. Show me Your invisible hand working in this family. Turn my eyes towards You.

Amen.

Bless the LORD, O my soul, And forget not all His benefits.

PSALM 103:2 NKJV

FATHER,

You remind me of what You've already accomplished.

I forget the past so easily. I ask for so much in prayer and then forget to say, "thank You," when You provide the answers. When discouragement crowds out joy in my life, help me remember the victories You've won, the prayers You've answered, the miracles You've performed. Your love never fails. Never. My feelings don't always reflect the reality of who You are and what You've done. Give me the power to move beyond my feelings into Your truth.

Amen.

Be strong, do not fear; your God will come.

ISAIAH 35:4

FATHER,

You are my Strength.

I feel like a disappointment to You, as well as to my kids and myself. I battle to be the person You want me to be. The closer I get to You, the fiercer the battle grows. A pure heart doesn't come easily, but You know that's what I long for most. Give me the strength to fight this battle again today. Remind me that You're the Champion who fights through me and for me. Revive my soul.

Amen.

Be joyful in hope, patient in affliction, faithful in prayer.

ROMANS 12:12

FATHER,

You help me persevere.

It feels like some things never change. I keep trying to be the person and the parent You want me to be, but I get so discouraged. Life is hard, but You are big. Never let me forget that. Help me rest in Your timing and not try to force things to work out the way I want them to. Let the hope of Your answers to my prayers fill me with joy, while I wait for the changes You've planned.

Amen.

•   •   •

When
I NEED ENDURANCE . . .

"Staying with it—that's what God requires."

MATTHEW 24:13 THE MESSAGE

FATHER,

Your love encourages me to keep going.

It's easy to give up when life hurts. That's what I want to do right now. I'm tired, discouraged, and longing to be somewhere, anywhere, other than here. But I know You've placed me here for this season of my life. That's reason enough for me to stay. But I want to do more than just go through the motions. I want to put my whole self into what You have for me today. Energize me with Your love.

Amen.

We are more than conquerors through Him who loved us.

ROMANS 8:37 NKJV

FATHER,

You declare me to be a "conqueror."

I'm just a weak woman—a mother filled with frailties and prone to mistakes, anger, and selfishness. But in You, I'm a conqueror—more than a conqueror! You enable me to be so much more than the person I see in the mirror. Strengthen me today. Cheer me on when I grow tired. Lead me to victory. Then may all of the glory go to You and You alone. May Your strength shine through my weakness, pointing the way to You.

Amen.

Whatever your hand finds to do, do it with all your might.

ECCLESIATES 9:10

FATHER,

You remind me of my work's eternal worth.

Some days I feel as though I'm going nowhere. There's always laundry to wash, dinner to cook, and kids to discipline for the same thing they did yesterday. I get tired of the repetition, the tediousness, the obscurity of motherhood. But You show me how everything I do is another way of worshiping You. Let me worship boldly and wholeheartedly. Let me see Your purpose in every task I do today, big and small. Let me offer only my best.

Amen.

We also rejoice in our sufferings, because we know that suffering produces perseverance; perseverance, character; and character, hope.

ROMANS 5:3-4

FATHER,

You provide perspective.

You're molding me day by day. You're chipping away at my pride. Slowly, but surely, You're turning me into a humble servant to You and to my children. When I grow tired of the process, show me how far I've come. Use what's wearing me down to smooth out the rough edges in my character. Help me put others first out of pure love, without resentment. Mold me into the woman You had in mind when You first created me.

Amen.

• • •

When
I FEEL EXHAUSTED . . .

"Come to me, all you who are weary and burdened, and I will give you rest."

MATTHEW 11:28

FATHER,

You help carry my burdens.

I'm not sure how I'm going to make it through today. All I want to do is crawl back into bed. The day ahead seems too heavy for me to carry, but I know Your shoulders are big enough to bear the burden. Let me lean on You, knowing that You never consider me a burden, but a blessing. What a joy it is to hear those words! I love You, Lord, not just for what You do, but also for who You are.

Amen.

> *You've kept track of my every toss and turn through the sleepless nights.*
>
> PSALM 56:8 THE MESSSAGE

FATHER,

You give me rest.

I've had enough of sleepless nights. Please free my mind from everything that's preventing me from getting a good night's sleep. Help me get the rest my body needs. Don't let me use exhaustion as an excuse to be cranky and impatient with everyone else. Use this season of my life to slow me down and to help me depend solely upon You. Show me what to do and what to leave undone. Then bless me with Your gift of sleep.

Amen.

*Ask where the good way is, and walk in it,
and you will find rest for your souls.*

JEREMIAH 6:16

FATHER,

You provide a vacation for my soul.

I'm so tired physically that it's affecting me emotionally, mentally, and even spiritually. You are my Refuge. Enfold me in Your refreshing presence. Be my Home away from home. Fill me with rest that goes deeper than a good night's sleep. Provide the energy I need to follow Your will, even when my body is aching. Show me how to take care of myself physically and still meet the needs of my children. Help me find balance in my life.

Amen.

Relax and rest. GOD *has showered you with blessings.*

PSALM 116:7 THE MESSAGE

FATHER,

You help me relax.

My body may be tired, but spending time with You always leaves me feeling more awake and alive. I can relax in the comfort of Your Spirit and the security of Your acceptance. The weariness of motherhood fades away as You rock me in Your arms. Your words are like a lullaby to my soul. My loving Father, come to Your child now. I need to know You're close. I need to know that I'm not doing this job alone.

Amen.

• • •

When

I FEEL LIKE A FAILURE . . .

It is God who arms me with strength and makes my way perfect.

2 SAMUEL 22:33

FATHER,

You are the only One who can make my way perfect.

I keep trying to live this life on my own. Worse yet, I expect myself to be able to do it perfectly. Forgive me for my pride. At least failure teaches my heart humility. Thank You for that lesson. Help me accept Your forgiveness and move forward from this place. Show me how to be a success in Your eyes, no matter what that looks like in the eyes of the world. Make me perfect in Your time and strength.

Amen.

Remember Your Creator.

ECCLESIASTES 12:1

FATHER,

You remind me that I'm Your child.

Every feature, every talent, every gift I possess was fashioned by Your hand. Even before my birth, You knew what my life would hold—all of my successes and failures, disappointments and victories. Teach me to accept and learn from them all. No matter what my emotions tell me, I'm still Your beloved child. I am Your masterpiece. Give me the strength of heart to try again. Help me grow into the woman and mother You desire me to be.

Amen.

*Each of you must take responsibility for doing
the creative best you can with your own life.*

GALATIANS 6:5 THE MESSAGE

FATHER,

You never give up on me.

I did my best, but I failed anyway. Still, that's all You ask of me—my best. Thank You for the comfort of Your grace. You never judge my success or failure by what others see but by what You know is in my heart. Take away my need to compare myself to others; they're not the yardstick by which I should measure my life. I need to measure it against You and Your will for me. Show me how to do that.

Amen.

Intelligent people are always open to new ideas. In fact, they look for them.

PROVERBS 18:15 NLT

FATHER,

You help me try again.

I blew it. My heart keeps condemning me with my failure. I know those are not Your words, but mine. Help me take a deep breath and start again. Show me what I need to learn, so I can do it right the next time. Open verses in Your Word that will give me insight and encouragement. Lead me to people who may have advice I can learn from. Then pick me up and give me a gentle push forward.

Amen.

•   •   •

When

I NEED FAITH . . .

"Don't look for shortcuts to God."

MATTHEW 7:13 THE MESSAGE

FATHER,

You are the One who helps my faith grow.

When my faith seems even smaller than a mustard seed, I need to see how big You are. Thank You for the gift of Your Word. Seeing how You've worked in people's lives throughout history gives me the courage to step out in faith further than I ever have before. Stretch me, Lord, even if it's uncomfortable. Help me continue to choose to spend more time with You. That's the only way our relationship and my faith will grow.

Amen.

The Lord, the God above all gods, is awesome beyond words.

PSALM 47:2 TLB

FATHER,

You show yourself worthy of my trust.

There is no one like You, Lord. You're a mighty Warrior who fights by my side. You're a caring Father who tends to my needs. You're a patient Counselor when I don't know which way to turn. You're a constant Friend when I feel all alone. You're an all-powerful King who deserves my adoration and praise. You're Lord over all You have created. There is no greater joy in life than to be loved by You.

Amen.

Devote yourselves to prayer, being watchful and thankful.

COLOSSIANS 4:2

FATHER,

You help me see with my heart.

It isn't easy trusting in Someone I can't see, but I want to, Lord. I don't want to be like Thomas, only believing in what I can see and touch. I know Your Spirit is present everywhere in this world and beyond. Help me to not only believe this with my head, but also with my heart. Help me to act on that belief, trusting in Your power and promises to accomplish what You've set before me, even if it seems impossible.

Amen.

If you do not stand firm in your faith, you will not stand at all.

ISAIAH 7:9

FATHER,

You help me stand firm.

Some days I act as though You don't even exist. I put my faith in my own feeble abilities. I trust others who are as flawed as I am to be perfect. I run in fear from situations that You're in control of. I want to give up on my kids when You refuse to give up on me. Forgive me. You remain faithful, even when my faith in You wavers. Give me the faith I need to stand firm today.

Amen.

• • •

When

I NEED HELP WITH MY FINANCES . . .

Unless the LORD builds the house, its builders labor in vain.

PSALM 127:1

FATHER,

You help me set my priorities straight.

So much of my time is spent making money, spending it, or wishing I had more. But my security isn't found in an ample bank account. It's only found in You. My financial state can change overnight, but You remain my faithful Provider. Give me wisdom to know how to handle what You have graciously given me. Teach me how to use it as a tool and not to worship it as the answer to my problems. I want to worship only You.

Amen.

We can make our plans, but the final outcome is in God's hands.

PROVERBS 16:1 TLB

FATHER,

You help make ends meet.

Just doing the bills leaves me feeling overwhelmed at times. Whenever we seem to be making a little headway, an unexpected expense appears out of nowhere. Lord, teach me how to spend, save, and give responsibly. Show me how to live within my means. When I compare my life with those around me, I always find myself stretching our finances further than they should go. Help me look at Your values, instead of the world's. Be my financial Planner.

Amen.

"It is more blessed to give than to receive."

ACTS 20:35

FATHER,

You teach me how to be a cheerful giver.

Everything I have is Yours. Just because a check has my name on it, instead of Yours, doesn't change whose money it really is. I want to follow in the footsteps of Your generosity. You've shown me that giving sacrificially isn't convenient or comfortable, but it is necessary. There are so many needs and so many chances to show love through my actions, instead of just my words. Help me let go of the grip I have on what You've freely given me.

Amen.

You brought us to a place of abundance.

PSALM 66:12

FATHER,

You bless me with more than enough.

Just like the Israelites wanted to hoard manna, I always want more than I need. Help me to be satisfied with what You've given me today, Lord. Thank You for giving me so much more than my "daily bread." Thank You for all of the extra blessings You've brought my way that are far above and beyond what my family can use today. Teach my children and me true contentment and gratitude, whether we have plenty or little.

Amen.

•   •   •

When

I NEED TO FORGIVE
MY CHILD . . .

Be patient with each person, attentive to individual needs.

---

1 THESSALONIANS 5:14 THE MESSAGE

FATHER,

You help me look beyond my emotions.

It feels like no one can make me as angry as my children do. Why is that, Lord? Is it because I love them so deeply or because they're my kids, that I expect them to be perfect—more perfect that I am as an adult? Help me stop and look at a situation before automatically reacting to it. Help me see beyond what's been done or said to see what You're doing in my child—and me.

Amen.

"This is My commandment, that you love one another as I have loved you."

JOHN 15:12 NKJV

FATHER,

You ask me to imitate You.

Your love is so deep and pure, while mine is so inconsistent, so conditional. As Your child, I know how often You've forgiven me. Show me how to do the same for my own children. I need to let go of the hurt that their defiance, disobedience, and disrespect bring to my heart. I know I've brought that same kind of pain to Your heart over and over again. Forgive me. Then help me forgive them.

Amen.

Discover beauty in everyone.

ROMANS 12:17 THE MESSAGE

FATHER,

You remind me of the treasure with which You've entrusted me.

This child is a gift straight from Heaven. Help me never to forget that, Lord. Help me to see the beauty You've woven into each individual, especially the ones You've put into my care. I know that life is a refining process. Help me not to hold my children up to impossible standards. Help me to recognize their weaknesses, pray for change, then celebrate growth. Help them become who You've designed them to be, not just who I envision them to be.

Amen.

Many waters cannot quench love; rivers cannot wash it away.

SONG OF SONGS 8:7

FATHER,

You teach me what true love is.

My anger gets in the way of my love. I don't want it that way. I want to be a mother who loves unselfishly, not just when it's easy. It wasn't easy for You to love me, but that love led Your Son to the cross. How can I believe I'd be willing to die for my kids if I can't even forgive the missteps they make along the way? Only You can teach me to be more like You.

Amen.

•   •   •

When

I NEED FORGIVENESS . . .

Clean the slate, God, so we can start the day fresh! Keep me from stupid sins, from thinking I can take over your work.

PSALM 19:13 THE MESSAGE

FATHER,

You wipe my slate clean.

I love You, Lord. It's so much easier to say those words than to act as though I really mean them. Thinking about the price You paid for what I've done puts my selfishness into perspective. I am so sorry. Please forgive me. Yet I know that before those words even leave my lips, You already have forgiven me. Your love and grace humble my self-centered heart. Change me from the inside out. Make me new, whole, and pure.

Amen.

The LORD longs to be gracious to you; he rises to show you compassion.

ISAIAH 30:18

FATHER,

You remind me that there's no limit to Your forgiveness.

No matter how many times I say, "I'm sorry," Lord, I find myself coming to You once again, filled with shame. I'm so stubborn and unteachable. Yet every time I come to You, Your forgiveness flows onto me as fresh and pure as if this were the very first time I'd failed. Your love truly is what leads me to repentance. Please show me how to forgive my children as willingly and lovingly as You have me.

Amen.

I will give you a new heart and put a new spirit in you; I will remove from you your heart of stone and give you a heart of flesh.

EZEKIEL 36:26

FATHER,

You change my heart.

But today my life doesn't seem any different from the lives of those around me who don't believe in You. I keep putting my own desires ahead of Yours. I go along with the crowd, choose what's easy, and shy away from sacrifice. But even though outward changes seem slow in coming, I know something has changed on the inside. I care about doing the right thing, about pleasing You. When I am weak, You do prove yourself strong.

Amen.

• • •

When

I NEED A FRIEND . . .

This I know: God is on my side.

PSALM 56:9 NLT

FATHER,

You are always on my side.

Sometimes I feel like an unwanted orphan. I long for someone to come alongside me and be my best friend— as well as protector, comforter, and counselor. Lord, You are the only One who can fill that hole in my life, and You fill every corner of it. Thank You for making me feel as though I'm worth spending time with. I know I can never bore You with my stories or call too late at night. I'm truly grateful.

Amen.

Offer hospitality to one another without grumbling.

1 PETER 4:9

FATHER,

You teach me how to be a friend.

The crazier my schedule, the pickier I am about who I spend my occasional spare moments with. Honestly, I think I want good friends who require low maintenance. But at the same time, I expect those same friends to meet my needs at a moment's notice. Lord, show me what it means to put others before myself and my needs. Teach me what true love looks like.

Amen.

I will sing to the LORD as long as I live. I will praise my God to my last breath!

PSALM 104:33 NLT

FATHER,

You are always home.

Right now, I could use a friend. Funny how I turn to You only as a last resort. Why is that? You're always available. You're ready to listen. You long to spend time with me. Somehow I even think You laugh at my jokes. You know me inside and out, and yet You still love me. And You'll never leave me, from the moment of my birth to my last breath and beyond. Who could ask for a better Friend?

Amen.

> *The LORD's loved ones are precious to him.*

PSALM 116:15 NLT

FATHER,

You are my true soul Mate.

I expect so much out of those around me—my friends, my kids, my spouse. But You are the only One who can fill every need. You treat me as if I were the only person in the world. You love me without any conditions, in spite of my weaknesses. Isn't that what I'm really longing for from everyone else? Help me bask in Your love. Then let that love spill from my life into the lives of others.

Amen.

• • •

When

I AM SEARCHING
FOR FULFILLMENT . . .

---

*When I awake in heaven, I will be fully sat-
isfied, for I will see you face to face.*

PSALM 17:15 TLB

FATHER,

You fill my deepest longings.

There are holes in my soul that can never be filled by
anything on this earth. There's nothing I can buy, no
exotic destination I can visit, no career title I can achieve
that will satisfy the emptiness I feel inside. This side of
Heaven, I'll never be fully satisfied. It's not until I'm with
You, face to face for eternity, that I'll know what real fulfillment feels like. That's the moment my heart will be
truly whole.

Amen.

> *Don't become so well-adjusted to your culture that you fit into it without even thinking. Instead, fix your attention on God. You'll be changed from the inside out.*

ROMANS 12:2 THE MESSAGE

FATHER,

You set my priorities in line with Your will.

When I look at other mothers, whether they're at the mall or on TV, so many of them seem to have their lives together. They seem so happy and fulfilled, and I start longing for what they have. But You show me the true meaning of fulfillment. You show me that who I am is more important than what I do, how I look, or what I own. My fulfillment comes from following You in all I do.

Amen.

Aspire to lead a quiet life.

1 THESSALONIANS 4:11 NKJV

FATHER,

You bring to mind my many blessings.

Being a mother isn't glamorous. It isn't filled with praise or recognition. Sometimes it's filled with frustration, disappointment, and even loneliness. But You've blessed me with the most important job on earth. You've given me children whom You have created in Your image—kids who have holes in their hearts that only You can fill. Just like I have. Help me find contentment, joy, and fulfillment in the life that You've given me, even when it's far from exciting.

Amen.

> *"Ask yourself what you want people to do for you, then grab the initiative and do it for them."*

MATTHEW 7:12 THE MESSAGE

FATHER,

You help me take my eyes off of myself.

When I long for greener pastures, show me what it means to put others before myself. I'm so worried about making sure my own needs are met and my own desires are satisfied. That's when I feel most discontent. Help me call off this pity party. Teach me how to love You with my whole heart, soul, mind, and strength and how to love others as I do myself. Most times, loving myself is the easy part. Show me how to spread that love around.

Amen.

•   •   •

When

I NEED GUIDANCE . . .

In all your ways acknowledge Him, And He shall direct your paths.

PROVERBS 3:6 NKJV

FATHER,

You help me make the right decision.

The only Map I have in this life is You. You show me which way to turn, in both big and small decisions. I don't want to rely on intuition, emotion, or even what everyone else is doing. I want to do what's best in Your eyes. Make the direction I'm supposed to take very clear to me, Lord. I want to make the best choice, not just a good one. Let Your Word and Your voice be my true guide.

Amen.

Each morning I will look to you in heaven and
lay my requests before you, praying earnestly.

PSALM 5:3 TLB

FATHER,

You give me more than good advice.

You've given me a blueprint for how I should live my life and raise my kids. Even though all of the details aren't written down—that would be too overwhelming to follow anyway—You've given me sound principles of love, sacrifice, and forgiveness. More than that, You've given me Your Holy Spirit so that these things can become more than principles. They can become realities in my life. My prayer is for the wisdom to apply what You've already given me.

Amen.

Keep your eyes open for GOD, watch for his
works; be alert for signs of his presence.

PSALM 105:4 THE MESSAGE

FATHER,

You are right here, leading me.

I don't know which way to turn, but You won't let me wander off aimlessly. Like a watchful parent, You always have a tight hold on my hand. I'm never out of Your sight. Guide me now. Help me move forward with wisdom and confidence. Even though I can't see the big picture, I know that step-by-step You're leading the way. Give me the courage to follow You, even when the path is narrow and lonely.

Amen.

Encourage one another daily, as long as it is called Today.

HEBREWS 3:13

FATHER,

You guide me through Your Word and Your people.

Sometimes Your voice comes across in a whisper, other times in a shout. A verse of Scripture, the chorus of a song, the words of a friend, the message at church, even the beauty of Your creation . . . everything testifies to who You are and to Your great love for me. Let me hear Your voice now. Every day is filled with choices that either draw my family and me closer to You or further away. Give me the wisdom to make the choices that will draw us ever closer to Your side.

Amen.

•   •   •

When

I NEED HEALING . . .

To you who fear My name The Sun of Righteousness shall arise With healing in His wings.

MALACHI 4:2 NKJV

FATHER,

You are the great Physician.

You know me inside and out. You created my body, and only You know how to heal it perfectly. That's what I'm praying for, Father. I know that physical healing isn't always the answer You bring to this prayer, but it is the longing of my heart. And I know that the cries of my heart rise to Your throne. Please bless me with the healing I long for. Give me relief. Help me rest in Your healing hands.

Amen.

Forget the former things; do not dwell on the past. See, I am doing a new thing!

ISAIAH 43:18-19

FATHER,

You heal me emotionally.

My heart aches. I'm constantly on the verge of tears. I don't know how I can be the mother I'm supposed to be when I feel like I'm dying inside. I want to hide away in Your loving arms, but I know I need healing, not just a hiding place. Help me face this pain in my heart. Uncover the wounds that need to be cleansed. I know that's not a painless process, Lord, but I'm ready. Heal me.

Amen.

I have loved you with an everlasting love; I have drawn you with loving-kindness.

JEREMIAH 31:3

FATHER,

You are the Worker of miracles.

You have made the blind see, the deaf hear, the dead rise again. You can heal broken bodies, broken hearts, and broken homes. You have the power to make every area of my life whole and healthy. I'm trusting You to heal me in the way that brings the most glory to You, in Your time and in Your way. That isn't easy to say, Lord. But I want to be wholly Yours. Only You know what that really looks like.

Amen.

Just as the sufferings of Christ flow over into our lives, so also through Christ our comfort overflows.

2 CORINTHIANS 1:5

FATHER,

You long for me to be made whole.

I need Your healing touch right now. I'm tired and hurting. I feel useless like this, needy. Is this right where You want me, Lord? I'm not sure. I'm almost afraid to ask. The only thing I'm sure of is Your love for me and Your desire to make me like You. Nothing can prevent You from working that miracle in my life. Show me what it means to share in Christ's sufferings, as well as His comfort.

Amen.

• • •

When

I NEED HOPE . . .

Those who went off with heavy hearts will come home laughing, with armloads of blessing.

PSALM 126:5 THE MESSAGE

FATHER,

You lighten my heavy heart.

No situation is hopeless in Your eyes. Please bring to my mind Your promises, Your love for me and my kids, Your power over the impossible, and Your eternal perspective. Help me look beyond the circumstances. I know You're still in control, just as You've always been. Give me the faith I need to hang on when things just don't seem to change. When all I can do is pray, Lord, let me know that is enough.

Amen.

May you overflow with hope through the power of the Holy Spirit.

ROMANS 15:13 NLT

FATHER,

Your Spirit provides the power I need.

I'm so thankful I don't have to handle this on my own. It's easy for me to give up when things don't go my way. I get discouraged. I lose sight of tomorrow. I begin to believe that if my best efforts have failed, there's nothing else that can be done. But Your Spirit comforts my weary heart. You provide the perseverance I need and the hope I long for. You help me make it through another day.

Amen.

Whatever I have, wherever I am, I can make it through anything in the One who makes me who I am.

PHILIPPIANS 4:13 THE MESSAGE

FATHER,

You are enough.

Why do I feel so hopeless, Lord? I want to run away, give up, disappear. But I know in my heart that You and Your power are all I need to face whatever happens in this life. Why do I doubt that? Help me take today one moment at a time. Let me relax in the peace of Your presence, finding confidence in Your purpose in my life. You are right here, right now, right beside me. Thank you, Lord.

Amen.

Those who are righteous will be long remembered. They do not fear bad news.

PSALM 112:6-7 NLT

FATHER,

You calm my fears about the future.

What kind of world is this, Lord? How can people do the things they do? Just reading the morning paper or watching the news can start the tears flowing. But I know that whatever happens to me or my kids isn't hidden from Your sight. You know what tomorrow holds. Your love is bigger than my fears. Help me do what is right no matter what is happening around me. Strengthen my heart in the face of evil.

Amen.

•   •   •

When

I FEEL INSIGNIFICANT . . .

> *O LORD, you are our Father. We are the clay, you are the potter; we are all the work of your hand.*
>
> ISAIAH 64:8

FATHER,

You carefully created me.

You chose every detail of my design. You chose where I was to be born and when. You chose the children I would raise. Even now, You're still molding me, shaping me, making my heart more like Yours. You're using my kids to help accomplish this purpose. Remind me that what really matters is who I am, not the tasks I accomplish. Let me be Your hands, Your feet, and Your voice to those around me.

Amen.

Many women do noble things, but you surpass them all.

FATHER,

You know a mother's worth.

You chose to bring Jesus to earth as a baby dependent on a mother's care. Mary's job was far from insignificant. But sometimes the monotony of doing the same tasks over and over again, day after day, makes me feel as though I'm not doing anything that really matters. Reveal to me the ways that I do make a difference in this world and in my kids' lives. Keep my heart satisfied with where I am and what I'm doing right now.

Amen.

•   •   •

When
I Am Jealous . . .

Don't compare yourself with others.

GALATIANS 6:4 THE MESSAGE

FATHER,

You don't compare me to others.

So why do I? I'm always measuring myself in the light of others' accomplishments, possessions, or appearances. Everyone else's kids seem more disciplined, their houses more put together, their marriages more satisfying, their wardrobes more flattering. Why do I keep trying to be someone I'm not? I'm not just discontent; I'm jealous. Forgive me. Help me change my point of reference and keep my eyes on You. Nothing can compare to the depth of Your love.

Amen.

> *I have learned the secret of being content in any and every situation.*
>
> PHILIPPIANS 4:12

FATHER,

You know that life isn't fair.

You know I don't get what I really deserve. Thank You for that, Lord! I deserve death, but You give me life. I deserve condemnation, but You give me grace. You bless me, not because I've earned it, but because You love me. Teach me how to rejoice in the blessings of others, as well as for all of the wonderful things You've done in my life. You are overwhelmingly generous. Teach me how to be unceasingly grateful.

Amen.

> *Am I now trying to win the approval of men,*
> *or of God?*

Galatians 1:10

Father,

You are the only true Judge.

But I keep trying to win the approval of those around me. That just leaves me feeling jealous that I don't have the advantages or natural abilities others seem to have. I feel like I don't measure up, because I feel as though I am not "enough." But I am enough in Your eyes. I've always had Your love. Because of Jesus, I even have Your approval. What more do I need to have or be?

Amen.

. . .

When

I NEED TO LET GO . . .

---

*The Fear-of-GOD builds up confidence, and
makes a world safe for your children.*

PROVERBS 14:26 THE MESSAGE

FATHER,

You hold my children's futures in Your hands.

I don't. That's not a mother's job. My job will never
be fully finished as a parent, but this phase of it has
now come to an end. You know my kids' weaknesses
better than I do. You know what troubles and tragedies
they'll face. And You'll be with them, just as You have
been with me, through every season of their lives. I
trust You to bring them to maturity in You. Protect
them. Bless them. Love them.

Amen.

The memory of the righteous will be a blessing.

PROVERBS 10:7

FATHER,

You've blessed me with wonderful memories.

Thank You for making my mind in such a way that I can hold on to my favorite moments and relive them again and again. Thank You for blessing my life with memories worth reliving. I'll always be a mother, but that role will look different as I enter this new phase. Help me celebrate this time of change. Give me wisdom to know how to make this transition a positive one. Open my eyes to new challenges. Teach me how to love from a distance.

Amen.

Where you are right now is God's place for you.

1 CORINTHIANS 7:15 THE MESSAGE

FATHER,

You keep me growing.

I've watched my kids grow, but I've often forgotten to watch myself do the very same thing. But it's time. Time for change. Time for growth. Time to let go and watch my kids soar on their own. Being needed less doesn't mean I'm loved any less, but sometimes it feels that way. Stop me from clinging to the past. Use me in new ways. Teach me how to grieve and rejoice at the same time.

Amen.

•   •   •

When

I LONG TO BE LOVED . . .

I can always count on you—God, my dependable love.

PSALM 59:17 THE MESSAGE

FATHER,

You are the Lover I long for.

You created my heart with a hunger for love, a thirst to be known. You created my heart to feel empty without You. Then why do I believe what I see in the movies? Why do I blame that ache in my heart on my husband's inattentiveness or lack of romance? Even if he were the perfect husband, he couldn't fill my need for true love, for Your love. When I feel that ache, Lord, lead me straight to You.

Amen.

Your love, O LORD, reaches to the heavens,
your faithfulness to the skies.

FATHER,

Your love can find me anywhere.

When I feel alone, forgotten, unappreciated, and unloved, Your almighty arms reach out to me. It doesn't matter where I am, in the quiet of my bedroom or the crowded aisles of the mall. You are there. You haven't forgotten me, even when it feels as though everyone else has. You haven't given up on me, even when I've disappointed those around me. You loved me before I took my first breath, and Your love will extend beyond my last.

Amen.

100 • *Everyday Prayers for Everyday Cares for Mothers*

Surely goodness and love will follow me all the days of my life.

PSALM 23:6

FATHER,

Your love for me cost You dearly.

True love involves sacrifice. It isn't easy or convenient. It's selfless and forgiving. Over and over You've proven the depth of Your love for me. Remind me of Your miracles of the past, Your answers to prayer, the integrity of Your character. Remind me of what true love looks like. It's the closest thing I have to a picture of Your face. I want to see that face, Lord. Show me how to love You the way You've loved me.

Amen.

> *"Make yourselves at home in my love."*
>
> JOHN 15:9 THE MESSAGE

FATHER,

You are my heart's true Home.

I don't need to woo You to win Your love, yet You continue to do just that for me. You are as attentive to me and my needs as a lovesick suitor. But Your love is pure, mature, sincere, and selfless. You shower me with gifts for no special reason. You see beyond my faults and declare me beautiful. Sunsets and answered prayers are all love letters from You. You're constantly reminding me that I'm loved—deeply, completely, eternally.

Amen.

* * *

When

I NEED HELP IN
MY MARRIAGE . . .

Two are better than one.

ECCLESIASTES 4:9

FATHER,

You said it wasn't good for people to be alone.

That's why You designed marriage. But sometimes I feel alone, even when I'm with my husband. Show me why I feel this way. Show me what expectations of mine are unrealistic or just plain selfish. Show me how to love him the way that You do. I know that two different people becoming one isn't an instant, easy process. But I need Your encouragement and wisdom to keep trying, Father. I need Your kind of love.

Amen.

An honest answer is like a warm hug.

PROVERBS 24:26 THE MESSAGE

FATHER,

You give me the courage to be honest.

Running away from problems is so much easier than facing them—at least for the time being. But Your Spirit won't let me run away forever. You keep drawing me back to fight for the marriage I know You want us to have. Being honest is risky, but I know You're working in my husband's heart, as well as my own. Give me the words I need to say. Then help me listen with my heart, instead of my emotions.

Amen.

God delights in those who keep their promises.

FATHER,

You are the Healer of relationships.

Heal ours. I'm tired, discouraged, and hurt. I get angry, and I am ready to pass the blame so easily. I know that with Your love there are no irreconcilable differences. But reconciliation and forgiveness are things that I can't do in my own strength. Let Your commitment to loving me be my example and Your words, my guide. I don't know how to love without expecting anything in return. Teach me what that looks like. Help me love like You.

Amen.

Everyday Prayers for Everyday Cares for Mothers • *105*

*This is my prayer: that your love will flourish
and that you will not only love much but well.*

PHILIPPIANS 1:9 THE MESSAGE

FATHER,

You are the Author of love.

I know that real love bears little resemblance to what I
see in the movies or on TV. I want a marriage built upon
true love, not fantasy. Teach me what the difference is,
Lord. I commit myself to pray for my marriage. I want it
to be built upon a solid foundation of Your love, no
matter how hard that is. Help me see my husband the
way You do. Reveal to me the things You love most
about him.

Amen.

•   •   •

When

I FEEL OUT OF
CONTROL . . .

*"You're blessed when you're at the end of
your rope. With less of you there is more of
God and his rule."*

MATTHEW 5:3 THE MESSAGE

FATHER,

You reveal my weaknesses.

What looks like frustration to me is a tool for You. When
my kids push me to my limit, You can use them to teach
me that my limits aren't large enough. Calm me down, so
I don't miss the lessons You want to teach me. Only You
are perfect and never lose control, but Your Spirit is alive
and moving in me. I want You to have more control over
my life, especially over my emotions. Slow me down.

Amen.

Kind words are like honey—sweet to the soul and healthy for the body.

PROVERBS 16:24 NLT

FATHER,

You keep me from sinning.

Only You know the evil that lies so close to the surface of my life. The littlest things can set it off. Stop me before it spills out onto my kids or anyone else. Help me close my mouth before I say words I can't erase. I want to be remembered for my kind words, not my angry ones. Show me what true kindness looks and sounds like. Slow me down enough to think before I speak.

Amen.

Let's not just talk about love; let's practice real love.

1 JOHN 3:18 THE MESSAGE

FATHER,

You help me mature.

I know I'm not a toddler anymore, but right now I feel like throwing a tantrum. Help! Stop me from dumping my frustrations on my kids. I want to do what You want me to do, to be the mother You want me to be, but I feel so weak and out of control. Lead me beside still waters, just as You've promised. Show me how to keep loving, even when everything feels like it's falling apart.

Amen.

•   •   •

When

I FEEL OVERPROTECTIVE . . .

Fear of the LORD gives life, security, and protection from harm.

PROVERBS 19:23 NLT

FATHER,

You are in control.

I know that I'm not, but I still long to protect my kids from harm. You, as a Father, know what that's like. Even though it's hard for my heart to believe, You love my children even more than I do. Only You have the power to keep them truly safe. Guard not only their bodies, but also their minds and hearts. Be their Place of refuge. Be mine as well. Help me find rest from anxiety in Your love.

Amen.

Let us draw near to God with a sincere heart in full assurance of faith.

HEBREWS 10:22

FATHER,

You are the perfect Parent.

I want to be that for my kids, but I have limits to how far I can help them. I don't have the power to make their lives easy and pain free. I can't see further ahead than the minute I'm living in right now. You know the future. You see the good that grows out of the very things I'm afraid of for my kids. Help me let go. I don't want to play God. You're the only One worthy of that job.

Amen.

•   •   •

When

I NEED PATIENCE . . .

Patient persistence pierces through indifference;
gentle speech breaks down rigid defenses.

PROVERBS 25:15 THE MESSAGE

FATHER,

You are patient with me.

Please help me be the same way with my kids. I know You forgive seventy times seven. I struggle with having to tell my kids something twice. Help me not to take everything so personally. I want to celebrate my kids' victories and be patient and loving when they fail. Even when they're outright rebellious, Lord, give me the strength and patient persistence to love them as You do. Take my impatience and turn it into prayer.

Amen.

When the way is rough, your patience has a chance to grow.

JAMES 1:3 TLB

FATHER,

You teach me what patience really means.

It's not an instant gift; it's a fruit of the Spirit that takes time to grow. I'm tired of things not going the way I want them to. I want my kids to do what I say, period. I want things to change this minute. But I'm still a work in progress, longing for the patience to learn patience. I'm thankful that Your patience is as endless as Your love. Use my children to make me more like You.

Amen.

If we hope for what we do not yet have, we wait for it patiently.

FATHER,

You teach me to wait.

I feel like a kid on a car trip asking, "Are we there yet?" I hate waiting for anything. What kind of example am I to my kids? My expectations for my kids and for how quickly You should answer prayer are much higher than my expectations for myself. I'm a slow learner, but I want to be a consistent one. Help me hold on to hope, even when what I long for isn't yet within my reach.

Amen.

114 • *Everyday Prayers for Everyday Cares for Mothers*

My times are in Your hand.

PSALM 31:15 NKJV

FATHER,

You hold time in Your hands.

You haven't given us eternal spring or summer. You've created our lives to have seasons. While I'm longing for the flowers of spring, You've blessed me with the beauty of snowfall. In Your very design of the world, You are teaching me to wait. My children took nine months of growing before I could see them face to face. Maturity will take a lot longer than nine months—for them and for me. Help me enjoy the seasons along the way.

Amen.

• • •

When

I Long for Peace and Quiet . . .

Be still before the LORD and wait patiently for him.

PSALM 37:7

FATHER,

You are my quiet Place in a busy world.

Life is so hectic right now that I feel I'm behind even before I get out of bed. Don't let the pace of my life cause me to lose sight of You. I'm here right now, listening and waiting. Show me how to be still. Teach me how to relax, without making this time yet another chore on my long list. I want to enjoy just being with You as I enjoy the company of my closest friends. No expectations. No demands.

Amen.

Better is one day in your courts than a thousand elsewhere.

PSALM 84:10

FATHER,

Your presence is like a vacation.

When my life feels crazy, there You are. You are my walk in the park when I can't get out of the house. You are my nap on the beach in the middle of piles of laundry. One heartfelt prayer, Lord, and the busy, rushed, stressful life around me fades away for a moment. Renew me now with Your energy and perspective. Quiet my heart enough to hear Your voice, no matter how loud my life gets.

Amen.

Mercy, peace and love be yours in abundance.

JUDE 1:2

FATHER,

You are my Peace.

It feels like everyone is demanding something from me, but all You ask of me is my love. Even then You never demand it. You wait patiently for it while continuing to pour Your love overabundantly into my life. That's what draws me to You more than anything else. I want to rest in Your goodness, to have a quiet spot in my heart that remains, despite a messy house and whining kids.

Amen.

•   •   •

When

I AM PRIDEFUL . . .

Acknowledge and take to heart this day that the LORD is God in heaven above and on the earth below. There is no other.

DEUTERONOMY 4:39

FATHER,

You alone are worthy of praise.

I'm proud of my kids. I'm proud of my accomplishments. I'm proud of how far I've come. These are all good things. They are all worthy of a pat on the back. But You are the only One worthy of being put on a pedestal. When I feel cocky, remind me of how small I am compared to You. Lead me back to the Source of my victory, and put all the glory right where it belongs—on You.

Amen.

You give me your shield of victory; you stoop down to make me great.

2 SAMUEL 22:36

FATHER,

You are the Victor.

You've made me who I am. You've blessed me with every one of my strengths and have helped me grow in every area of weakness. Everything I've accomplished, every victory I've had, has come more from Your hand than from my own. Teach me to be happy with who I am without putting myself above others, especially You. You humbled yourself by becoming human, so I could have the chance to become eternal. Never let me lose sight of that.

Amen.

•   •   •

When

I NEED HELP WITH
MY PRIORITIES . . .

---

*A pretentious, showy life is an empty life; a
plain and simple life is a full life.*

PROVERBS 13:7 THE MESSAGE

FATHER,

You teach me about the abundance of simplicity.

You've shown me treasures that I don't have to dust or make payments on. But it's still so easy to get distracted by what I can hold in my hands, by what my neighbors have, or by what I see on TV. What I see with my eyes can never fill my heart. Thanks for reminding me of that when I forget. Help me find a balance between my needs and my wants. Teach me the joy of true contentment.

Amen.

May he give you the desire of your heart and make all your plans succeed.

PSALM 20:4

FATHER,

You help me put my life in order.

But right now it just seems so upside-down. There are so many things that are fighting for my time and money, not to mention my heart. I need Your wisdom to sort them out, to weigh them in light of eternity. Even the little things, Lord. Sometimes those are the ones that pile up high enough to prevent me from doing what's really important, like spending time with my kids, just loving them without an agenda.

Amen.

LORD, remind me how brief my time on earth will be.

PSALM 39:4 NLT

FATHER,

You know how long my life will be.

Show me how to use it well. It seems silly to pray over a To Do list, but that's exactly what I need. Help me make the most of the day that You've set before me. I want to choose to do what's best over what's simply good, nice, or even most urgent. When the time comes to meet You face-to-face, I want You to be able to say, "Well done, My good and faithful servant." I know that I need Your daily help in order for that to happen.

Amen.

If your wealth increases, don't make it the center of your life.

PSALM 62:10 NLT

FATHER,

You are my heart's Treasure.

I love Your blessings. I'm grateful for all You've given me that's beyond what I really need. But, my priority is to have more of You in my life, not more stuff. I don't want my fickle heart to fall more in love with the gift than the Giver. Draw me closer to You. Help me let go of everything that I treasure more than You. I'd rather be poor in possessions and rich in Your presence. Show me how be in Your presence.

Amen.

•   •   •

When
I Feel Stressed . . .

As pressure and stress bear down on me,
I find joy in your commands.

Psalm 119:143 NLT

Father,

You are the Source of joy.

I keep thinking if I can just make it through this phase or finish that project, my life will slow down. But something new always seems to come up. I know motherhood is often a juggling act, but I feel like too many plates are in the air. Show me which ones to get rid of, even if I have to let them drop and break. Give me joy in the juggling. Remind me that I'm never facing this alone.

Amen.

"In this world you will have trouble. But take heart! I have overcome the world."

JOHN 16:33

FATHER,

You know what my day holds.

My stomach ties itself in knots just thinking about it, but that isn't how You want me to face trouble. You want me to let You carry the burdens that I keep trying to lug on my own tired shoulders. You've had victory over much greater troubles than these. I know You'll show me how to face whatever lies ahead, one moment at a time. Right now, Lord, I'm putting all my troubles in Your mighty arms.

Amen.

Cast your cares on the LORD and he will sustain you.

PSALM 55:22

FATHER,

You relieve the pressure inside me.

You take what feels like an impossibly heavy weight and replace it with Your peace. I need that relief, Lord, that release. So, one by one, I'm casting my cares on You. Not one of them is a surprise to You. Heal the burdens of my heart. Help me put aside the worries that I never should have picked up in the first place. Free me up to be the mother my kids need, the woman You created so carefully.

Amen.

The One I've trusted in can take care of what he's trusted me to do right to the end.

2 TIMOTHY 1:12 THE MESSAGE

FATHER,

You care about the details.

You know everything that's weighing me down right now. I know that You never give me more than I can handle, but I keep trying to handle everything on my own. That was never what You had in mind. When I reach the breaking point, I am finally reminded of that, Lord. My life is crowded with more than You ever planned for it. Help me sift out the things that I don't need to solve, fix, or carry.

Amen.

•　•　•

When

I FEEL THANKFUL . . .

Is anyone happy? Let him sing songs of praise.

JAMES 5:13

FATHER,

You set my life to music.

You know the deepest longings of my heart and are so creative in how You fill them! Thank You for the countless blessings You shower on me, just because. There are no words I can speak that are sincere enough, deep enough, or rich enough to express my gratitude. Let this song of praise that keeps echoing through my heart never stop. May it be a sweet sound around Your throne that makes You smile.

Amen.

I'm happy from the inside out.

PSALM 16:9 THE MESSAGE

FATHER,

Your joy runs deeper than my circumstances.

My life isn't perfect. It isn't even easy. But today I feel such a satisfying sense of happiness that I know it can't have come from anywhere but Your hand! Thank You for that simple pleasure. Let me savor every drop. Stop the everyday frustrations of motherhood that grate on me from the outside from distorting the gratitude I feel on the inside. Let this joy flow from my life out onto my kids.

Amen.

From the fullness of his grace we have all received one blessing after another.

FATHER,

You are gracious.

You give and give and give. You are the kind of parent I want to be. Help me be generous with my own kids. I don't want to lavish them with gifts as much as I want to lavish them with love. Help me be generous with my time and words of praise. Teach me how to give from a full, unselfish heart. Make me an honest-to-goodness blessing in their lives. I want my kids to see You in me.

Amen.

I have God's more-than-enough, More joy in one ordinary day Than they get in all their shopping sprees.

PSALM 4:7 THE MESSAGE

FATHER,

You answer prayers I haven't yet prayed.

You know my heart better than I do. You know what I long for and strive for, as well as what I'm afraid of and rejoice in. You shape my life, even the ordinary days, with tenderness and creativity. The joy of just knowing that I'm loved every day of my life, and beyond, is something I can't even put into words. But Your understanding of me goes so much deeper than what I say. Eternity isn't long enough to express my thanks.

Amen.

•   •   •

When

I NEED MORE TIME IN MY DAY . . .

Teach us to number our days, That we may gain a heart of wisdom.

PSALM 90:12 NKJV

FATHER,

You help me make every minute count.

The days fly by. I feel like I'm always busy, but some things just never seem to get done. Help me choose wisely how to use the twenty-four hours that You've given me today. Make me sensitive to my kids' needs, knowing when to stop and spend time just listening or giving a hug, even if the kitchen isn't clean yet. Help me use today in a way that honors You with a balance of work, play, and praise.

Amen.

Don't burn out; keep yourselves fueled and aflame.

ROMANS 12:11 THE MESSAGE

FATHER,

You help me balance work and rest.

Every night I go to bed with the feeling of having left things undone—yet another reminder that I can't do this job alone. I need Your energy to do what has to be done during this crazy time of life, and I also need Your wisdom to know what to leave undone. Help me be efficient, yet flexible. When I'm overwhelmed, let me rely on You to be my Shot of caffeine, as well as my Place of rest.

Amen.

●　　●　　●

When

I'm Facing a Tragedy . . .

I weep with grief; encourage me by your word.

PSALM 119:28 NLT

FATHER,

You are my Comfort.

Thank You for the gift of tears. How else could I express everything I feel inside right now? I want to turn back time, to make things like they were, but I know that life keeps moving forward. Show me how to move forward as well. I need Your strength to keep going, to be the kind of mom my kids need right now. I don't understand why this has happened, but I trust You and Your love. No matter what.

Amen.

Disaster strikes like a cyclone and the wicked are whirled away. But the good man has a strong anchor

PROVERBS 10:25 TLB

FATHER,

You are the only One who can dry tears from pain this deep.

I don't even know what to pray, but I trust that You know just what I need. I feel like life is falling apart, but I know that You're still in control. I still believe in Your power, love, and faithfulness. Show me how to hang on to the truth of who You are when life just doesn't make sense. Show me what faith under fire looks like. Then please use me to help others find Your comfort in all of this.

Amen.

• • •

When

I FEEL UNAPPRECIATED . . .

"If anyone wants to be first, he must be the very last, and the servant of all."

MARK 9:35

FATHER,

You see everything I do.

You know how hard I work at being a good mom, wife, and friend. I don't do it for recognition, but I wouldn't be honest if I didn't say how far gratitude goes in making me feel appreciated. Right now, I just feel taken for granted. I don't want those feelings to grow into resentment. Show me how to get rid of this hurt in my heart, these angry words in my head. Show me what servanthood really means.

Amen.

If you are really wise, you'll think this over—
it's time you appreciated GOD's deep love.

PSALM 107:43 THE MESSAGE

FATHER,

Your favor is all the reward I need.

I know I've done what You have wanted me to do. I've been faithful in my job as a mom. At least I've tried to do the best I can with Your strength. But no one seems to notice, except You. Let that be enough, Lord. Let the sound of Your voice whispering, "Well done, My good and faithful servant," be the only reward I long for, the only words of appreciation I need. Use me as You see fit.

Amen.

A woman of gentle grace gets respect.

PROVERBS 11:16 THE MESSAGE

FATHER,

You teach me humility.

So often I feel like my kids, wanting to cry out, "Look at me! Look at me!" when I've accomplished something I'm proud of, even if it's just making it through a mountain of laundry. But You show me the beauty of a humble heart. Balance my pride with humility. Help me find true joy in accomplishing what You've set before me, regardless of whether or not others take notice or say, "Thank you."

Amen.

•   •   •

When

I FEEL UNATTRACTIVE . . .

"You're blessed when you're content with just who you are—no more, no less."

MATTHEW 5:5 THE MESSAGE

FATHER,

You are my Designer.

You take pride in who You created me, in every feature both inside and out. Where the world looks at me with their eyes, You see me first with Your heart. You never compare me with the women in magazines. Please stop me from doing that very thing. Take my eyes off the mirror and the scale. Help me find the beauty that You see in me. Help me relax and be exactly who You created me to be.

Amen.

Even to your old age and gray hairs I am he,
I am he who will sustain you.

ISAIAH 46:4

FATHER,

You watch me as I age.

I have really changed since I had kids. I see it. I feel it. And I really don't like it. But You see every gray hair and the beginning of every wrinkle. You know every ache, even the one I feel when I look in the mirror and don't like what I see. Teach me how to love myself as much as You do. Help me remember that my worth is found in who I am, not in how I look.

Amen.

Each of us is an original.

GALATIANS 5:26 THE MESSAGE

FATHER,

You bring out the beauty in me.

The longer I know You, the more comfortable I am in my own skin. Help me be responsible in taking care of this body that You've designed just for me. But at the same time, prevent me from comparing myself to the women around me. Show me how to praise You for the way I am "fearfully and wonderfully made," for my uniqueness, for Your originality. The more I understand Your love for me, the more beautiful I feel.

Amen.

. . .

When

I NEED WISDOM . . .

Prepare your minds for action.

---

1 PETER 1:13

FATHER,

You prepare me for action.

Your wisdom is like aerobics for my mind. Your laws and words of love are just what I need to get in shape to do the right thing at the right time. Today show me how to apply what I've learned. Push my own pride and opinions out of the way. Slow me down enough to wait for Your insight and direction before I act. Then give me the strength to go forward in boldness.

Amen.

Show me Your ways, O LORD; Teach me Your paths.

PSALM 25:4 NKJV

FATHER,

You are the Source of true insight.

Your guidance is more than intuition; it's a light in the darkness. You see the right way to turn in every situation. Help me see that way now. I get so confused by my emotions, by my own sense of helplessness, that I feel lost. You are my Compass. In this very moment, be my true North. Help me rest in knowing that You are a trustworthy Guide. Guide me now in righteousness, decisiveness, and love.

Amen.

We never really know enough until we recognize that God alone knows it all.

1 CORINTHIANS 8:2-3 THE MESSAGE

FATHER,

You are infinitely wise.

I know that mothers are supposed to know it all, but this one sure doesn't. I can read all the best books on parenting, get great advice from friends, and still fail. Only Your wisdom, founded in love and grace, can lead me forward as a mother. That's what I'm asking for, longing for, Lord. Do what it takes to make me a woman of wisdom. This moment, give me the insight I need.

Amen.

Love wisdom like a sister; make insight a beloved member of your family.

FATHER,

Your words are my guide.

But I don't want to rely on what I've learned in the past, though You've taught me a lot. Every morning, encourage me turn to You and Your Word. Help me grow in wisdom and love. Take what's in my head, plant it deeply into my heart, and then use it to help me become the mother my children need. Help me live what I believe in a way that will be a lifelong blessing to those around me.

Amen.

•   •   •

When
I Am Worried . . .

"Who of you by worrying can add a single
hour to his life?"

MATTHEW 6:27

FATHER,

You know every outcome.

I don't, but that doesn't stop me from worrying about what I can't control. Set my mind free from this useless cycle. If I should do something, help me do it. If there's nothing I can do, then let me rest in knowing prayer is enough. I trust in You and Your love, but I still struggle with the uncertainty of life, especially when it comes to my kids. Help me place them in Your hands, moment by moment.

Amen.

Instead of worrying, pray. Let petitions and praises shape your worries into prayers, letting God know your concerns.

PHILIPPIANS 4:6 THE MESSAGE

FATHER,

You shape my worries into prayers.

It's sure better than letting those worries tie my stomach into knots. Thank You for leading me to Your throne, for letting me climb into Your lap and tell You about everything that troubles my heart. You never brush me off, making light of my concerns. Even when You don't give me the answers I long for, You comfort me with Your love. You're gentle and mighty. You're powerful enough to handle my concerns, yet tender enough to calm my fears.

Amen.

*If anything is excellent or praiseworthy—
think about such things.*

PHILIPPIANS 4:8

FATHER,

You ease my mind.

You wipe away my worries and replace them with words of thanks. You provide a peace that makes no sense in light of the circumstances, except for the fact that You're in control. You've proven yourself worthy of my trust over and over again. When I lose sight of You in the midst of everything that's going on, remind me of Your faithfulness. Help me see You as You really are, as King, Creator, Comforter, Counselor, and Lord.

Amen.

I call as my heart grows faint; lead me to the rock that is higher than I.

PSALM 61:2

FATHER,

You calm my heart.

Today it's hard for me to see Your hand in everything that's going on, but I know it's there. You won't let go of my kids or me no matter what the future holds. You know what I long for, how I want everything to turn out. That's my prayer to You, the honest plea of my heart. But You know what's best in light of the big picture, which I cannot see. I trust in the wisdom of Your will.

Amen.

• • •

When

MY CHILD IS AFRAID . . .

God is a safe place to hide, ready to help when we need him.

PSALM 46:1 THE MESSAGE

FATHER,

You are a safe hiding Place.

I know what it's like to be afraid. It makes me feel so helpless and small. That's how my child feels right now. I can't calm my child's fears, but I know You can. Be a safe Place where he/she can run and hide. Replace anxiety and sleeplessness with the peace of Your presence. Give me wisdom, words of comfort, and a way to help my child learn how to turn to You whenever fear begins to take hold.

Amen.

I will not be afraid, for you are close beside me, guarding, guiding all the way.

PSALM 23:4 TLB

FATHER,

You are a Night-light in the darkness.

You chase away everything, imagined or not, that's filling my child's heart with fear. Make yourself known to him/her in a special way right now. Take away the worry and anxiety. Replace it with Your strength and perspective. Let Your light reveal the truth about what he/she is truly afraid of. Then show my child how much bigger You are. Help me understand what I can do to give him/her a clearer picture of You.

Amen.

•   •   •

When

My Child Is Angry . . .

> *"You're blessed when you can show people
> how to cooperate instead of compete or fight.
> That's when you discover who you really are,
> and your place in God's family."*

MATTHEW 5:9 THE MESSAGE

FATHER,

You bring reconciliation.

Teach me how to be a peacemaker. Keep my own heart calm and rational, even when my child's is not. I don't want to just ignore this mood, hoping it will go away. I want to deal with it in Your way, in Your timing. Please provide me with what I need to do that, Lord. Prepare my child to hear my words and be receptive to my actions. But no matter how he/she reacts, help me to do what's right.

Amen.

A gentle answer turns away wrath, but a harsh word stirs up anger.

PROVERBS 15:1

FATHER,

You are gentle with Your children.

Help me be the same way with mine. Teach me how to respond to their anger without snapping back. You know that's rarely my first response. I want to lash out, to have the last word, to get even if I've been hurt by my own children's words. All that does is make things worse. Don't let me sink to their childish level. Help me rise closer to Yours. Give me the right words and motives.

Amen.

Love is patient, love is kind.

1 CORINTHIANS 13:4

FATHER,

You know what's behind my child's anger.

You know whether he/she is hurt, embarrassed, prideful, or just plain tired. Give me insight into what's behind the frustration. Show me how to deal with the root of the anger, not just the inappropriate outbursts. Give me the patience and self-control that I need to be kind in return. If my child's been treated unfairly, help me see this clearly and deal with it appropriately. Help me exemplify Your love to my child.

Amen.

•   •   •

When

MY CHILD IS DEPRESSED . . .

May the God of hope fill you with all joy and peace.

ROMANS 15:13

FATHER,

You bring hope out of despair.

Some problems in my child's life are too deep for me to fix. This is one of them. I want to do more than just raise his/her spirits; I want to fill my child's heart with hope. But You are the only One who can work that miracle. That's what I'm asking of You now. Lift this dark cloud that's settled over my child's heart. Fill him/her with Your peace, even when life is hard.

Amen.

No mind has conceived what God has pre-
pared for those who love him.

1 CORINTHIANS 2:9

FATHER,

Your love can reach my child.

My love is not enough, no matter how much I'd like it to be. I hurt for him/her. I'm not sure of where to turn, other than to You. I'm desperate for Your wisdom. Guide me in the right direction to find help that can break through this depression. Thank You for always being there for me and for my child. Hold him/her close right now. Protect him/her from retreating any further. Make Your love known.

Amen.

In Your presence is fullness of joy.

PSALM 16:11 NKJV

FATHER,

Your presence is my child's true home.

Break down these walls my child has built around his/her heart. Right now, I think You're the only One who can get in. Replace this hopelessness with the comfort and joy that come from being close to You. Give my child a deeper understanding of Your love. Let it wash over him/her like a refreshing stream, bringing with it a renewed sense of hope, purpose, and self-worth. Where there's sadness, replace it with joy.

Amen.

. . .

When

MY CHILD IS
DISAPPOINTED . . .

I will pour my Spirit into your descendents and my blessing on your children.

ISAIAH 44:3 THE MESSAGE

FATHER,

Your blessings never end.

Help my child get beyond this disappointment. I know it's a deep one. Help me not to treat it too lightly or dwell on it more than I should. Give me words that will soothe the hurt. Give my child perspective beyond his/her years. Help him/her see this loss in light of all the blessings that You've brought our way in the past. You've been so good to every one of us in this family.

Amen.

In you our fathers put their trust . . . in you they trusted and were not disappointed.

PSALMS 22:4-5

FATHER,

You never disappoint us.

Thank You for Your faithfulness to my children and me. You never promise something and then fail to fulfill it. Help me be as faithful and honest to my kids as You've been to me. Let me never be silent about Your blessings and answers to prayer. I want to feel free to thank You openly and jubilantly in front of my kids. Help them understand that though life may disappoint them, You never will.

Amen.

Be cheerful no matter what; pray all the time;
thank God no matter what happens.

1 THESSALONIANS 5:16 THE MESSAGE

FATHER,

You help my child see beyond this moment.

You can pass on Your perspective, even to the smallest heart. Show my child how to get over this disappointment, how to find joy in what's going right, instead of dwelling on what's not going as planned. I know You can take the deepest disappointment and bring something good out of it. Please do that now. Help my child grow and forgive, then find comfort, and even joy, where disappointment used to be.

Amen.

•   •   •

When

MY CHILD NEEDS DISCIPLINE . . .

Be tender with sinners, but not soft on sin.

JUDE 1:23 THE MESSAGE

FATHER,

You model mercy.

You're both loving and just at the same time. You're the role Model I need when it comes to discipline. Show me how to follow in Your footsteps as a parent. Give me the wisdom I need to apply what I already know. It's such a fine line between being too hard on my kids and too soft on them. Help me to find that balance when it comes to setting boundaries and then enforcing them when they're broken.

Amen.

He who answers before listening—that is his folly and his shame.

PROVERBS 18:13

FATHER,

You give me wisdom.

You help me judge right from wrong. Please do the same for my child. Let Your Holy Spirit be heard clearly in both of our hearts. Open my ears not only to Your voice, but also to what my child is saying behind his/her words. I need to know whether this is a matter of immaturity, testing, habit, rebellion, or just a stupid mistake. Help me choose carefully what to do and say in this situation.

Amen.

Discipline your children, and they will give
you happiness and peace of mind.

FATHER,

You've placed this child in my care.

You've given me the responsibility of raising him/her in a way that reflects Your character as a Parent. I know that consistent discipline yields rewards over time, but right now I'm tired of fighting the same battles over and over. Give me the strength and perseverance to continue doing what's best for my child. Give me creativity in how I deal with this. Guard my heart from anger and discouragement. Encourage me with Your promises for my child's future.

Amen.

All of our praise rises to the One who is strong enough to make you strong.

ROMANS 16:25 THE MESSAGE

FATHER,

You give me victory.

I'm sorry when I think of how often I treat Your discipline of me as lightly as my child does mine. But I'm so grateful to You for giving me a picture of how a loving Parent should act. Bring that picture to mind whenever I feel like giving up—or blowing up. Take these prayers and use them to strengthen my attempts to discipline my child. The ultimate victory is in Your hands, not mine.

Amen.

•   •   •

When

My Child Is Disrespectful . . .

Show proper respect to everyone.

---

1 Peter 2:17

Father,

You are worthy of respect.

I, however, am not. But You've created us to respect one another and give honor to our parents. Do I? Am I expecting more from my child than I expect from myself? Reveal the sin in my own heart before I react to my own child's so strongly. Give me the grace to show my child respect, not because he/she has earned it, but because love demands it. Then help me address my child's disrespect in a Godly way.

Amen.

Parents are the pride of their children.

PROVERBS 17:6 NLT

FATHER,

You've given me authority over my children.

Help me be worthy of the respect You ask them to give me. I want to be a mother they'll be proud to point out to their friends, but I also want to be more than a friend. I need to use the authority You've given me to help them mature. You know how much cutting words hurt me. I don't want to react out of pain but teach out of love. Give me the wisdom to know the difference.

Amen.

The godly think before speaking.

PROVERBS 15:28 NLT

FATHER,

You help me forgive.

You know my child's tongue and actions are out of control. I can discipline him/her, but I can't change my child's heart. You know how desperately it needs changing, Lord. I'm not only frustrated by my child's actions, I'm also embarrassed. His/her disrespect seems to label me as a bad parent. Help me not to take this battle so personally. Season my communication with wisdom, grace, and kindness, no matter what words or actions are aimed at me.

Amen.

•   •   •

When

MY CHILD FAILS . . .

Even though on the outside it often looks like things are falling apart on us, on the inside, where God is making new life, not a day goes by without his unfolding grace.

2 CORINTHIANS 4:16 THE MESSAGE

FATHER,

You love us unconditionally.

You watch us fail, over and over again, but You never give up on us. You keep encouraging us to mature and grow, even when change comes slowly. Help my child understand this in his/her own life. Help my child not to feel like a failure just because he/she has failed in this one thing. Give me words of encouragement, not of comparison. Help me be a cheerleader, as well as comforter, knowing the right time for each.

Amen.

The wise person makes learning a joy.

FATHER,

You are a wise Teacher.

You know it takes both success and failure to make us the people You want us to be. Show me how to lead my child to the lessons You want to teach him/her in all of this. You know how I want to fly in and rescue my child when things get tough, but that doesn't help him/her grow. Give me the strength to allow my child to fail, to learn from the consequences of his/her own actions.

Amen.

• • •

When

MY CHILD NEEDS FAITH . . .

Babies not yet conceived will hear the good news—that God does what he says.

PSALM 22:31 THE MESSAGE

FATHER,

You've known my child longer than I have.

Your love and care far surpasses anything I can provide. You know my child more intimately than I ever will—every breath, every thought. You know how deeply he/she truly believes in You. I can only judge by the words I hear and the actions I see. My prayer is that this child will see You more clearly with every passing day. Give him/her a generous measure of faith and then help it grow.

Amen.

Teach a child to choose the right path, and when he is older he will remain upon it.

PROVERBS 22:6 TLB

FATHER,

You've made me a spiritual leader.

As a mother, I need to point this child in Your direction. You've asked me to walk alongside him/her, to lead, to pray, to encourage, to discipline, and ultimately, to let go. I can't lead my child in a direction I'm not going. Continue to draw me closer to You. Show me how to walk beside my child without dragging or lagging behind. Give me the boldness, integrity, and humility I need to be a worthy guide.

Amen.

Great is Your faithfulness.

LAMENTATIONS 3:23 NKJV

FATHER,

You are a sure Foundation.

You are the One and only God, the first and last, the almighty Creator. Your love reaches to the heavens and Your faithfulness to the skies. May Your Spirit also reach deep into my child's life. Keep tugging at my child's heartstrings, pulling him/her closer to You. Let his/her faith grow independent of my own. I know I can trust that the faithfulness You've shown to me, You'll also show to my child.

Amen.

When I pray for you, my heart is full of joy.

PHILIPPIANS 1:4 TLB

FATHER,

You call me to pray.

Talking to You changes things. I don't quite under-stand how, but I know it does. And change is what my child's heart needs right now. Thank You for giving me something I can do when I feel as though nothing can be done. Thank You for giving me the privilege of bringing my requests to You, so I never give up hope. Thank You for continuing to love me and my child, from birth to death and beyond.

Amen.

•   •   •

When

My Child Wants to Give Up . . .

FATHER,

You are the Strength my child needs.

Discouragement and disappointment have stopped my child in his/her tracks. My words aren't enough to keep him/her going, but Yours are. Speak to my child in the way he/she understands most clearly. Please provide the mental, physical, and emotional energy that my child needs to try again. Relight that passion that once was there. Provide friends with words of encouragement. Simply be the loving God I know You are.

Amen.

Let us run with perseverance the race marked out for us.

HEBREWS 12:1

FATHER,

You are an Encourager.

You're a Cheerleader for every one of Your children. You stand on the sidelines, shouting words of love and hope, which inspire us to keep going, even when the course ahead is rough and uncertain . . . even when victory is far from sure . . . even when we try to block out the sound of Your voice. Let my child hear Your voice so clearly right now. Give him/her the strength and courage to move forward.

Amen.

•   •   •

When

MY CHILD IS GRIEVING . . .

The LORD is close to the brokenhearted.

PSALM 34:18

FATHER,

You mend broken hearts.

I wish I could heal my child's heart, soothe the ache, dry every tear. But that's Your job, Lord. Be close to my child right now. I know this is hard for him/her to understand or even believe it's true. I feel the same way, but my faith in You has had so much longer to grow than my child's. I grieve, but I have hope. Fill my child with that same hope—Your peace that goes beyond understanding.

Amen.

As a mother comforts her child, so will I comfort you.

ISAIAH 66:13

FATHER,

You have a mother's touch.

You hurt right alongside every child of Yours, old or young. Bring Your tender comfort to my child's deepest hurt. Your heart is like mine towards my child, only truer, more faithful, more patient, more pure. You don't take his/her tears lightly. Give me wisdom on how to be Your arms during this time. Help me know just the right words or touch that will bring the greatest comfort, the deepest healing.

Amen.

• • •

When

MY CHILD IS ILL . . .

Nothing in all creation is hidden from God's sight.

HEBREWS 4:13

FATHER,

You know the cure for every illness.

You know every inch of my child's form, every cell of his/her body. You know what he/she needs to be healed. I ask for that healing now. I come before you humbly, knowing Your power and standing in awe of Your mystery. I know miracles don't happen every day, but that doesn't mean they don't happen at all. I'm asking for a miracle, but most of all, I'm asking for Your will to be done in my child's life.

Amen.

Because he bends down and listens, I will pray as long as I have breath!

PSALM 116:2 NLT

FATHER,

You care about our physical needs.

You've told me to come to You with any concern, big or small. Few things are as precious to me as the health of my children. Please bring relief and healing. Give me the wisdom to do all that is humanly possible; then help me rest in knowing You're in control. Bless my child with comfort, rest, and freedom from worry. Thank You for caring about each and every prayer I pray. Help me wait patiently for Your answer.

Amen.

• ❄ •

When

MY CHILD NEEDS PROTECTION . . .

Be to me a protecting rock of safety, where I am always welcome.

PSALM 71:3 NLT

FATHER,

You are a Rock of safety.

Your presence provides peace in the midst of danger. Your power is a shield of protection from harm. Nothing can happen without Your knowledge and consent. Right now, my child needs to know the safety of Your shadow, the comfort of Your arms. Please build a wall of security around my child. Don't allow anything to harm him/her physically, mentally, emotionally, or spiritually. Be a safe House for us all.

Amen.

God's angel sets up a circle of protection around us while we pray.

PSALM 34:7 THE MESSAGE

FATHER,

Your angels are near.

You are the Lord of the heavens and the earth. Countless angels surround Your throne, worshiping You in all Your glory. I can hardly imagine what that picture of beauty and power must be like! I know there are battles going on that I can't see with my eyes, battles that angels take part in. Take part in this battle before us right now. I pray You would encircle my child with protection.

Amen.

The LORD protects those of childlike faith.

PSALM 116:6 NLT

FATHER,

You treasure little children.

Your Son made a point of making time for them and of encouraging grown-ups to have faith like theirs. My child is Your treasure, as well as mine. You protect what You treasure, and You safeguard what is of immeasurable worth. Thank You for being a strong Tower for him/her right now, a Place of refuge and safety. Thank You for being there when I cannot, for guarding my child with Your mighty hand.

Amen.

•   •   •

When

MY CHILD IS
REBELLIOUS . . .

*If you love someone, you will be loyal to him
no matter what the cost.*

1 CORINTHIANS 13:7 TLB

FATHER,

You teach me what true love means.

Right now my child is anything but easy to love. Sometimes, I don't even like him/her. I never knew how a parent could feel this way until now. My feelings won't stop me from loving him/her, but I need Your strength and perseverance. I'm torn between anger and despair. Give me a glimpse of hope. One tiny breakthrough would be enough. I know You can do the impossible. That's all I have to hang on to right now.

Amen.

> *Wise discipline imparts wisdom; spoiled adolescents embarrass their parents.*

PROVERBS 29:15 THE MESSAGE

FATHER,

You impart wisdom.

That's what I need most right now. I feel as though I've tried everything, but nothing is working. If any of this is my fault, show me where I need to change, what I need to do, and what I need to say. I don't want to overreact just because of what other people will think. Give me real wisdom in understanding what is rebellion and what is nothing more than my child struggling to grow up.

Amen.

Forgive the rebellious sins of my youth.

FATHER,

Your grace is endless.

There's nothing my child can do that will turn Your love away from him/her. I struggle with forgiveness, but Your love is the example I cling to. Lavish Your grace upon my child right now. Lead my child to relationships that will draw him/her closer to You. Help me not to judge his/her rebellion too harshly or to ignore my own rebellion against You, no matter how subtle it may be. Thank You for Your boundless grace to us both.

Amen.

Do your best, prepare for the worst—
then trust GOD to bring victory.

PROVERBS 21:31 THE MESSAGE

FATHER,

You are my only Hope of victory.

At times I feel my child's situation is hopeless. It feels like I'm fighting a battle that I have no hope of winning. But with You, Lord, there's always hope. I need Your direction to know what I should do next. Help me release these worries that are choking the joy out of my life. Keep my heart tender toward my child. May my words be loving and my prayers consistent. Be my child's Guide, Protector, and Lord.

Amen.

•   •   •

When

MY CHILD NEEDS WISDOM . . .

Even a child is known by his actions, by whether his conduct is pure and right.

PROVERBS 20:11

FATHER,

You help me apply what I know.

Please do the same for my child. Take the knowledge he/she already possesses, and then give my child the wisdom and discretion needed to apply it to life. Let maturity and integrity win out over foolishness and impulsiveness. Give my child the desire to follow You, no matter what those around him/her are doing. Purify my child's heart and mind, revealing to me what I can do to help keep them pure.

Amen.

How can a young person live a clean life?
By carefully reading the map of your Word.

PSALM 119:9 THE MESSAGE

FATHER,

You are a trustworthy Guide.

Your Word is a flawless guidebook, pointing the way toward You and true life. Let Your words echo loudly throughout my child's life. Even if he/she isn't carefully studying Your Word, let what my child has heard in the past take root in his/her heart. You've promised that Your Word will never return to You void. Fulfill that promise now. Guide my child toward wisdom and away from lies that would lead him/her the wrong way.

Amen.

The Lord will guide you continually.

ISAIAH 58:11 TLB

FATHER,

You walk beside my child.

You're always with him/her. You never nag or belittle. You are the perfect Teacher, the flawless Parent, and the Source of true, pure wisdom. Nurture my child with Your never-ending love. Break down any barriers my child has built against You. Guide his/her decisions and guard his/her actions. Thank You for meeting my child's needs in a way that I never could, for staying right by his/her side long after my child has outgrown this home.

Amen.

Dear child, if you become wise, I'll be one happy parent.

PROVERBS 23:15 THE MESSAGE

FATHER,

You are a wise Mentor.

You raise my child right alongside me. You know his/her strengths and weaknesses. You know where my child lacks the judgment he/she needs to walk with integrity and love. Help my child grow in these areas. As my child matures, protect him/her from the mistakes that are bound to be made along the way. Keep me from becoming bitter or judgmental when my child acts foolishly. Mentor me in unconditional love.

Amen.

•   •   •

Additional copies of this book and other
titles from Honor Books
are available from your local bookstore.

Everyday Prayers for Everyday Cares
Everyday Prayers for Everyday Cares for Women
Everyday Prayers for Everyday Cares for Parents

If you have enjoyed this book,
or if it has impacted your life,
we would like to hear from you.

Please contact us at:

Honor Books
Department E
P.O. Box 55388
Tulsa, Oklahoma 74155
Or by e-mail at *info@honorbooks.com*